Praise for *The U*

MW01067479

"*The Unfolding* is the most powerful poetry collection I have ever read on grief and hope. With a language so deeply fluent in love, Rosemerry Wahtola Trommer takes us into the deepest depths of what it means to be human—the beauty and the pain woven together seamlessly. I have long admired Rosemerry's work. This is her most urgent collection yet. What a blessing to have read this masterpiece. What a privilege to walk in an era where Rosemerry Wahtola Trommer is writing and filling our lives with her beautiful, essential words. *The Unfolding* is a collection I am recommending to every poetry lover and reader I know."

    —Nikita Gill, author of *The Girl and the Goddess* and *These Are the Words: Fearless Verse to Find Your Voice*

"I don't know how she does it. In *The Unfolding*, Rosemerry Wahtola Trommer opens her arms and heart and voice so wide, everything we experience comes inside to be held, to shine. The greatest grief, our unexpected nudges of memory, the way the world goes on despite everything—she finds a way to weave continuance, embodiment of love, which may change shape, but never disappears. 'After I did not die the first minute, / I lived the next minute. / More truly, life lived me.' These powerful poems are anthems of clarity and ultimate care."

    —Naomi Shihab Nye, Paterson Poetry Prize recipient and author of *Everything Comes Next*

"I didn't realize how much I needed Rosemerry's words to remind me of what most matters. This beautiful collection of poems reveals the power of saying Yes to life, the blessings of loving without holding back. Each offering is a powerful transmission: our spirit is invited forward to cherish—praise!—both the darkness and luminosity of existence. Especially in these shadowy times, *The Unfolding* is pure medicine for our tender, awakening hearts."

    —Tara Brach, mindfulness teacher and author of *Radical Compassion*

"More than anyone I have ever encountered, poet Rosemerry Wahtola Trommer meets each moment with unbridled curiosity and then, after paying close attention to all its contours, takes that moment into her arms and praises it. She praises quietly or full-throated, with equal measures of humility and authority, down to the darkest bones and out to the luminous edges of the known universe. This collection reconfigured me."

    —Mirabai Starr, author of *Wild Mercy* and *Ordinary Mysticism*

"Like so many, I turn regularly to the work of Rosemerry Wahtola Trommer when I need to believe again that the world is still a kind and welcoming place, alive with compassion and full of singing even in the darkest of times. From the very first poem of hers that I read, I was led more deeply into myself, suddenly feeling that so much was possible, the field wide-open once more. In this latest collection, *The Unfolding,* her words become 'searchlights / that will help us find / what we don't yet know / we are looking for,' teaching us how to hold sorrow and beauty, grace and grief at the same time. Rosemerry Trommer is a fearless poet of the heart, and she possesses the exceedingly rare ability to turn even the simplest of moments into sacred lessons we can carry into our days, helping us to recognize—even when we'd rather turn away—the holiness that keeps unfolding at the center of our own very human lives."

— James Crews, author of *Unlocking the Heart: Writing for Mindfulness, Courage & Self-Compassion* and editor of *How to Love the World: Poems of Gratitude & Hope*

"*The Unfolding* re-opens our hearts and consciousness to the beauty of life and love, even amidst the shadows of devastating loss. Trommer warmly welcomes us into her orbit by offering us a glimpse into her most intimate memories and where we, too, can see ourselves and our own experiences. She fosters a loving solidarity for those who are searching for connection, particularly in the aftermath of loss. If you are searching, this is where you—your love, your bewilderment, and your aches—belong."

— Joyal Mulheron, Founder of Evermore

"The individual poems are brilliant and beautiful, but also the book as a whole works as a praise-song for the world, the lives we've been given, and the brief time we have to hold those we love. Very rarely do I see a collection so consistently wonderful as this one."

— Michael Simms, Founding Editor of *Vox Populi*

"Rosemerry Trommer's new collection of poems is saturated with dark beauty. There is an exquisite ache inside these poems, reminding us of the eternal embrace of love and loss. Trommer blesses us with what she has gleaned from her prolonged vigil in the underworld, revealing a language riddled with a vulnerability that pierces our hearts. *The Unfolding* breaks us open to what it means to be human, what it means to love."

— Francis Weller, author of *The Wild Edge of Sorrow: Rituals of Renewal and the Sacred Work of Grief*

THE
Unfolding

Rosemerry Wahtola Trommer

for Eric, Vivian, and Shawnee

Books and Audio by Rosemerry Wahtola Trommer

———

All the Honey (Samara Press, 2023)

Dark Praise (Sweet Tooth Records, 2023)

Hush: Poems (Middle Creek Publishing, 2020)

Naked for Tea (Able Muse, 2018)

Even Now (Lithic Press, 2016)

The Less I Hold (Turkey Buzzard Press, 2012)

The Miracle Already Happening: Everyday Life with Rumi
(Liquid Light Press, 2011)

Intimate Landscape: The Four Corners in Poetry & Photography
(Durango Herald Small Press, 2009)

Holding Three Things at Once (Turkey Buzzard Press, 2008)

Suitcase of Yeses (ARPIPE Records, 2007)

Insatiable: Poems (Sisu Press, 2004)

The Nature of Love (ARPIPE Records, 2002)

If You Listen: Poems & Photographs of the San Juan Mountains
(Western Reflections Press, 2000)

Lunaria: Poems (Sisu Press, 1999)

Contents

iii

Oh say, poet, what is it that you do?
                    —I praise.
But what of the deadly and monstrous,
how do you endure all this, how do you take it in?
                    —I praise.
But the nameless, the anonymous,
how, despite it all, do you keep calling to them, poet?
                    —I praise.
Where does it come from, your claim to be true
in every guise and in each mask?
                    —I praise.
And that the stillness and turbulence
know you like star and storm?
                    —Because I praise.

—Rainer Maria Rilke (1921)

PRELUDE

The poems in *The Unfolding* were all written since 2021, the year in which my son Finn chose to take his life and my father died of kidney failure. It's no surprise these losses now inform my everything. Perhaps you, too, have had the shelter of your heart splintered and leveled, leaving you naked and raw in the aftermath.

I've been surprised by what's been emerging from a broken and ransacked heart: A growing fluency with love. An ever-evolving intimacy with the sacred. A sense of communion with others who have also faced loss. Grief is so different for everyone. For me, it's been steeped with paradox. I've been companioned by these lines from Gregory Orr: "Not to make loss beautiful, / but to make loss the place / where beauty starts. Where / the heart understands for the first time / the nature of its journey." That gorgeous, impossible invitation shapes everything about this book.

Most of the poems in this collection aren't explicitly about loss, but they've all been written in the key of grief, composed in that tender threshold space we inhabit after loss. At the same time, the poems are undeniably songs of praise—for the ways we open, for love and beauty and wonder, even for grief and how efficiently it invites us to embrace our humanness and the mysteries of our relationships with each other and the divine.

My editor, Mark S. Burrows, suggested I consider Rainer Maria Rilke's call to praise as an organizing principle for this collection. I felt a full-bodied *Yes*, but what a challenge! I was immediately struck by the paucity of words for praise in English. As the Benedictine monk and author Brother David Steindl-Rast, OSB, writes, "when a word is lacking in a language, there is some insight lacking."

It seems we might be lacking insight here around praise. Our word "compliment" sounds transactional. "Commend" feels military. "Approve" connotes judgment. "Recommend" sounds commercial. "Extol" and "laud" feel highfalutin'. I wanted nuanced words that honored the grime and grace that are inextricably woven into our lives. Words that wrestled with how we might fall more deeply in love with the world even while we break and ache.

And so, in the spirit of one of my favorite books, John Koenig's *The Dictionary of Obscure Sorrows*, I blended ancient prefixes and roots to create the kind of layered lexicon I longed for and used these words as the section heads.

An example of how this play works: Consider *omenohymn* [oh-**men**-*uh*-him], derived from the Latin *omen*, "foreboding augury," and the late Latin *hymnus*, meaning "song of praise." I fancy it refers to the kind of praise that rises out of a moment simultaneously charged with radiance and darkness, fear and blessing.

This collection springs from such a moment. It was mid-August of 2021. My husband Eric, daughter Vivian, son Finn and I were in Georgia helping my parents move into their new retirement community. After a day of unpacking boxes and assembling furniture, Finn and I went for a midnight walk and took in the world around us, laughing till tears streamed down our cheeks. We spoke, too, of deep pain. The world seemed to mirror our conversation.

GRACE

What a loss it would be
to not have been born so
I would have missed
a Thursday night such as this
in which my son and I
walk the dark streets
in Georgia and watch
the lightning transform
the sky into pink flares
and smell some sweet
unnamable flower and
talk about Dodge Chargers
and knees and roaches—
I swear it has all been
worth it, every second
of fifty-one years, for this
hour in which there
are no bells, no shoulds,
no other tugs except
to take the next step
down the centerline,
while in the distance
raps another clap
of thunder.

That night was equally fueled by beauty and instability. I was thrumming with it. How clearly I felt the invitation to say *Yes* to the world as it was. Two days later, my son was dead, and yet the invitation remained. Almost three years later, that invitation to say *Yes* to the world as it is inspires every poem in this collection: The call to accept our vulnerability. To be curious. To open ourselves to love. To dwell more fully in the body. To feel how ephemeral all our epiphanies are. To live into the blank pages of our lives where new poems wait to be written. To praise what is. To be in service to the continual unfolding that is the nature of, well, everything.

Rosemerry Wahtola Trommer
Placerville, Colorado
July, 2024

I

VERILUJAH

––––––––

n. the praise that rises when we are in a state of raw, naked honesty,
aligning with the vast mystery of life as it is
instead of clinging to our story
about how we think life is supposed to be

from Latin *verus* (true) + *hallelujah,* song of praise
pronounced [ver-*uh*-**loo**-y*uh*]

SELF-PORTRAIT AS TUNING FORK

I am what continues.
—Joi Sharp

There is, perhaps you've felt it,
a moment when the day falls away
and your name falls away and

everything you thought you knew
falls away and for a moment
you know yourself only

as whatever it is
that continues—
your whole body abuzz

with the eternity of it—
and you quiver
as if struck by the great hand

of what is true,
becoming pure tone,
a vibration, a wave,

a human-shaped resonator
tuned to the frequency
of life itself,

and though later you might try
to dissect what happened,
in that moment you're too abloom

to wonder how or why,
you simply are
this ecstatic unfolding

knowing the self as *I am*,
so alive and so infinite
you tremble like a song.

Why I Stay Up Late Walking

At night I walk. Because
it is easier then to not
be my story. Easier to be
more flesh and less brain.

Easier to be the one
who is gathered into
the field of darkness
by night's great hands

and planted there.
Because sometimes
rain and sometimes wind
and sometimes stars

and always the world
so much larger than I,
so much vaster
than a small room

with a narrow doorway
and a tale relentlessly sad.
I walk not so much from,
but not so much to—

more that I walk through—
my ribs and lungs
becoming ladder rungs
that form a path

between earth and sky,
and I am more breath
than blame, more step than
shame, more now than why.

4

SOME NIGHTS MISSING YOU

is like the letter that doesn't come,
the one I would carefully slit open and slowly unfold,
then hold against my chest for a moment

before letting my eyes take in the first line,
the second, the rest, the last,
the letter that would explain everything

in language so plain
it would make my hands shake
with the truth of it,

the one that would arrive with a return address
so I would know where to respond if I dared,
the handwriting even, familiar, easily read,

with no pages missing, no passages indecipherable,
the letter that never once has arrived,
a letter I know only by its absence.

And the emptiness itself becomes faithful.
And the mystery becomes the only signature I trust.

TALKING WITH MY DAUGHTER ABOUT GRIEF

We lie in the dark
and speak about anything
but what I ache to speak about.
Some part of me longs
to find the words like searchlights
that will help us find
what we don't yet know
we are looking for.
Or a black light
that might help us see
what is valuable right here
but invisible to our ordinary eyes.
I try to infuse my words
with candlelight, but somehow
even this feels too brash,
too aggressive, and so
we lie in the dark
and I let the moon
do all the talking.
Oh waning crescent,
you know when to shine,
when to simply be held
by the dark.

You Belong

The way grass belongs to the meadow—
how without it, the meadow
would not be meadow—
this is the way you belong in my heart.
Not that I've made a space for you here,
more that you've helped make my heart what it is,
and without you, my heart is not my heart.

I cradle you here as in a nest of wheat—
soft home, humble home, ever rewoven
to fit the changing shape of you.
It's not true our hearts are our own:
they're symbiotic as meadows in spring.
The heart exists for who grows in it.
Who am I? Who am I?
You, my sun, my grass, my wind.

TOWARD PEACE

Perhaps some part of me still believes
peace is a destination,
a place we arrive, ideally together.

I notice how shiny it is, this belief,
like a flower made of crystal,
beautiful but lifeless,

devoid of the dust and scuff
that come from living a real day.
Meanwhile, there is this invitation

to grow into peace the way real flowers grow—
from dirt into air. With blight
and drought, beetles and hail.

Meanwhile this invitation
to live in the tangle of fear and failure,
to be humbled by my own inner wars

and wonder how to find a living peace
right here, the peace that arrives
when we take just one step through the mess

toward compassion and notice,
as our foot rises, our heart also rises
and in that lifted moment,

still scraping along in the dirt,
there is a peace so real we become light,
become the momentum that is the change.

THE VOW

What if this is all we get of heaven?
                        —James Crews, *"Small, Good Things"*

And if this is it,
this night
with its scent
of lawn newly mown
and the undammed river
high in its banks
and the baby bunny
eating every pansy
I just replanted,
yes, if this is it,
this kind voice
that returns
to tell me
I am enough,
though mostly
I doubt such truth,
if this is it,
the penstemon
blooming purple
and the cottonwood fluff
piling thick in every corner
and my desk a mess
with work I can never
hope to finish
and the loss
that is relentlessly sad,
if this is it,
then yes, I say,
I am here for this,
here, between the ache
and the sweeping
flight of the swallow,
here, between
the fallen tree
and the laughter
that won't stay in;
if this is it,
I would do it all again.

ACCEPTANCE

Today grief is a long steady rain
and the thing to do is to walk
in the long and steady of it.
The thing is to let the face
get wet, let the clothes get wet,
let the hair get wet and plastered
against the cheeks, the neck.
The thing is to meet the soaking world
and the soaking skin and the soaking
shoes and the soaking dreams
and not pretend it's dry.
Whatever longing there is for dryness,
it is soaking too. Because it's raining,
the thing to do is to walk in the long
and steady rain, to walk in the sodden,
soaking world, to trust that it will
not rain forever, to breathe in the scent
of the wet, wet earth, to kiss the rain,
to be kissed by the rain.
To be wet in the wet, wet world.

THE NAKED HEART GOES INTO TOWN

The heart walks down the street
with its big brim hat, its sunglasses,
its four chambers stepping up
onto the curb. It hopes it doesn't
run into anyone it knows.
It's hard enough to keep pumping,
pumping, one hundred thousand times a day.
That's all the heart can manage right now.
No conversation. No small talk.
No big talk. The heart has nothing to say—
a heart is made to feel,
and feel it does as it makes its way
to the post office, stops at the crosswalk,
feels it all.
Feels the cool breeze that buffets it.
Feels love for the scent of autumn,
love for the low-glancing light.
And it grieves for the loss
of what it once pumped for.
Grieves for the boy who still
lives in its walls. Grieves for
all who grieve, who weep.
Oh the heart, it feels so exposed
as it stands at the door of the coffee shop,
wonders if it can go in.
The other hearts in the coffee shop
seem to wear so much skin.
The heart sniffs at the dark and bitter scent,
remembers what it was like
to go inside, sip a coffee, talk about weather.
It pounds against itself,
walks on down the road.

KALSARIKÄNNIT

Finnish: Loosely glossed as the feel-
ing when you are going to get drunk
home alone in your underwear—
with no intention of going out (pro-
*nounced **kahl**-sahr-ree-**kan**-eet).*

Let's say a woman worked in the garden all day
pulling up old kale and bolted chard and harvesting
potatoes and garlic and onions, and let's say
her whole evening plan is to stay home
and shower and not get dressed,
and sip on a glass of wine or whiskey
until she is sweetly light-headed,
well, wouldn't it be lovely if there were a word
to describe her aspirations? A word
she could write in her calendar to be sure
no other loud plans swooped in. A word
she could say if her friends called and asked
what was happening tonight. And if
no one should call, she could say it to herself
for the joy of saying it—*kalsarikännit*—
as she toasted the air, clinking her glass
against all that isn't there.
And the wind on her skin, so brisk.
And the wine, so heady, so dry.

SMACK DAB IN THE MIDDLE OF A THURSDAY

Why do I resist calling it a miracle, this light
that in eight minutes and twenty seconds
has travelled ninety-three million miles

through solar wind particles and radiation
and countless numbers of solar neutrinos
to land here on my living room floor?

As if because it can be measured
and tracked it is any less divine.
As if, just because it's been happening

for four point five billion years
it is any less extraordinary,
this journey of warmth and radiance.

I let the light-loving animal of my being
curl into the spaces of the room
where the sunlight pools in bright welcome,

and I soften, soften into the wonder
of being alive in this very moment
in this very body with this very heart

meeting with very gentle amazement, this:
even as the heart breaks and burns,
bliss.

WILDING

—for Corinne

It is always near-freezing,
this high alpine lake where
we slide into oddly blue water,

and bare, strangled sounds
tear from our throats
as if our own wildness

is shredding through
manicured versions of self.
I crave it, this scraping away

of everything that isn't
limb-thrash and lung-gasp
and skin-scream and heart-bang

and wild uncontrollable breathing,
crave the tingling after,
the feral laughter, the way

the world slips more deeply into us
when we dare to slip
more deeply into the world.

HYMN

The shocking tender curl of him,
　　wild river, raging rush of him,
　　　the eddied, lazy swirl of Sunday
　　morning sleepy smile of him,
the flood-stage leaping wave of him,
　　high overflowing shores of him,
　　　torrential reckless course of him,
　　　　now empty, unfilled banks of—
　　dry barren rocky bed of—
　the utter lack of here of—
the pray-for-rain parched air of him,
　　dark growing rain cloud storm of him,
　　　the sometimes-I-hear-rapids hum,
　　　　deep currents in my lungs of him
　　　　　how is it I still breathe him in—
　　　the river is inside me hymn.

After Peeling the Beets

I resist peeling beets,
hate wearing their red tint
on my hands,
but today, the thought
of sweet roasted beets
was enough to make me
overcome my reluctance.
Later, I notice it is impossible
to feel separate and alone
when my hands wear the evidence
of what they've touched.
I find myself wishing
everyone could see on my skin
how my life has been marked by you,
how everywhere we touched
I wear the stain of love.

THE PARTNERS

—for my husband

After thirty years, she knows
he will speak with his mouth full.

He knows her stomach will gurgle
in the silence before they sleep.

He will set the table.
She will water the plants.

He will wash the windows.
She will dust the piano.

After thirty years, she still thrills
when he sits close on the couch

and rests his head on her shoulder,
then sighs aloud and closes his eyes.

She loves when the moment lasts.
In the mornings, he will look at the clouds

and tell her the direction of the wind,
what it means about the storm.

She will walk up to him with open arms
and hold him there, in the middle

of the kitchen. There will be no music.
It may look as if they are standing still,

but it's part of a long and intricate dance,
a dance they are still learning,

a dance no one else can teach them.
See how they step back, how they spin,

how they step in toward each other again.

For the One Who Is Gone

The way skin loves the scar
that remakes the skin into itself,
that is the way I love you.

I love you the way I love
driving on dirt backroads,
the way I love walking in the dark,

unsure of where I am,
unsure of where I'm going,
so the slightest movement

requires my whole attention.
I love you, though I am
a barren peach tree

with nothing to offer
but the memory of when
there were peaches, ripe and sweet.

And love is a glove
filled with holes
that still fits.

And love is a fountain
that doesn't care how many
coins are tossed in for wishes.

I love you the way I love the space
where the cottonwood used to stand—
how the air there will forever be

the place where the cottonwood grew.
I love you the way
the rain barrel loves the rain

that doesn't fall.
I love you because not loving you
feels like the worst fate of all.

SUNDAY AFTERNOON

Balanced together on a paddleboard
my daughter and I float across the pond.
Already we've splashed and tipped
and swum and squealed.
Already we've followed dozens
of blue dragonflies with our eyes
and greeted crawdads that cling to the reeds.
We've wrestled and tussled
and dunked and dried and now
we lie on our backs and glide
in the late August sun.
Warmth seeps into our skin.
She tells me stories
while I close my eyes,
and I think, *This is why I'm alive.*
If the moment is somehow made sweeter
because we've been intimate with death,
that is something seen only in retrospect.
For this now, we are sunbeam and story
and the tickle of damselflies
that land on our skin.
We are the aimless drift
from light to light.

When the Ambush Comes

You might be standing in line at the bank,
perhaps taking out the trash after midnight,
the moon somehow too bright.

If you can predict the quick tears,
the tight throat, that's not the ambush.
That's just grief.

The ambush comes when you're laughing.
Or when you're eating popcorn on the couch.
Or when you drive by a parking lot

where once you practiced parallel parking
with the one who is no longer here.
The ambush might come when you've just

put on mascara. Or when you're talking
on the phone to customer service.
Or when you're dusting the piano

where your loved one once sat
and practiced the theme
to *Pirates of the Caribbean*

over and over and over. And over.
And then you're crying again.
Not that you mind it.

Not that you're surprised.
You don't even apologize anymore.
This is what happens now.

It's what love looks like. You call it life.

Warning Label

In the small print that doesn't appear on my wrist
when you shake my hand, it says, *Not advised*
for those with low tolerance to weeping. It says,
For those allergic to intimacy, low dosage recommended.
It says, *Close contact is associated with a high risk*
of being included as a subject in poems.
Oh, blah, blah, blah. Everything comes with a warning label
these days. So many potential risks when we connect.
Like irrational happiness. Like loss. Like grief.
Like a deepening love that will never go away.

Choosing the Sorrow

In my heart today, a river of love for you—
sparkling, clear, easy to wade in.
Some may not understand
why I sometimes reach down
to pick up a smooth stone of sorrow,
not because I have stumbled on it,
but because I want to know its weight again.
I search beneath the glossy currents,
and always I find what I seek.
There are thousands of such stones,
enough to cover the whole river bed.
Every one of them precious.
Every one of them, a memory
of how it was to love you when you were alive.
Stone of you waking in your crib, pointing to light.
Stone of you doing tricks on your bike.
Stone of hiking up cliffs. Stone of dishes undone.
Stone of your eyes. Stone of long fingers.
Stone of you whistling across the room.
The river of love is no less powerful
for all this sorrow. When I am still,
often I choose to go wading here.
I notice how beautiful they are, all these stones,
worn as they are by the currents of love.
I notice how the current never stops.

STILL HERE

After I did not die the first minute,
I lived the next minute.
More truly, life lived me.
More truly, the thick air,
infused with lake scent and
rosemary and late summer
insisted I breathe. More
that the sun did not let me
not see the beloveds still here.
The thick green leaves
of August reminded me
life pushes through.
There was not a half-second
I forgot the horror.
And still I did not die.
After I lived the first day,
I lived the next,
opened the door and
drove the car and held close
the people I love.
Rain fell and a rainbow
bloomed and the night
was sleepless and long.
And longer. I lived the next week.
The next. The next.
I lived the next year.
And the next. More truly,
the same life that lives
through mushroom, tulip,
magpie, worm, eagle, gnat,
that same life keeps living me.
The horror, no less real.
And love continues to sprout
like new trees after fire.
Slow, and indisputable. All gift.
What seemed gone is still here.
The way light and dark and
air are still here. Another
day. Another year.

How To Meet This Difficult Day

Some days when I forget how to pray,
if I listen with my whole body

the world reminds me how
what is used up and spent
is also a vessel for the holy

as dry leaves become a nest,
as bare branches hold the sunrise.

It's Like This

"The odds of you being alive are basically zero."
—Dina Spector, reporting the work of Dr. Ali Binazir
(Business Insider, *June 11, 2012*)

It's like this: the sun itself
is constantly moving through space,
wherever and whatever that is,
and yet it never leaves us.
Add this to the list of marvels—
like how a glass of water
was once a cloud,
like how love can grow in us
despite despair, fear.
Given such gifts,
one must wonder how it is
our arms aren't constantly raised
in spontaneous praise for life.
I know and you know
why sometimes our hands stay down.
But now, standing still together,
even as we're spinning
and racing through space,
even if it's only a whisper,
when faced with the truth
that great forces hold
our lives in place,
it feels right to say
thank you, thank you,
eyes lifting, heart trembling,
the improbable earth
so solid beneath our feet.

II

SORROM

———

n. a paradoxical praise for beauty, love, strength and connection that can
only emerge as we wrestle with devastation, grief and
the worries and pains of daily living; a positive side-effect of
surrender and trust in life and death

from *sorrow* + *om* (from Hinduism and Buddhism),
originally indicating assent or agreement, pronounced **[sawr-**om]

Condition

My body, thank you for carrying this ache,
for carrying it not like a burden, but like a baby—

like a gift, like something that will
change you and keep changing you forever.

Of course you would want to shut down,
to close, to contract,

but I see how the grief grows you.
Though it shreds your sleep,

though it drops you to the floor,
you learn what it is to be human.

Through no effort of your own,
you are on board for a miracle.

So big, this invitation to love. Oh body,
you would never ask for this, and yet

you meet this grief every moment.
You find inner doors you never knew were there

and you swing them open, not to rid yourself
of the ache, but to grant it full access,

to know the grief completely,
to let it rewrite you, remake you, rebirth you,

to let it teach you what it means
to be alive.

How the Healing Happens

Again today
I dig with my teaspoon
into the soil
of sorrow.
It is said
there is healing water
somewhere below.

Perhaps I wished
for a shovel.
Perhaps there was
no shovel to be found.
Perhaps I did find a shovel,
but the work was
too heavy, too hard.

It is not hard
to dig one teaspoon
at a time.
Anyone can do it.
The hole gets wider,
deeper. At some point,
it feels like a well.
It is easy work.
It's the hardest work
I've ever done.

I thirst.
Yet what heals us
is not only
the promised water.
What heals is
the work itself,
dry and slow,
one spoonful,
and another spoonful,
and another parched spoonful.
And another.

WordWoman Joins the MCU

Long after the Avengers have obliterated Thanos
and Ant Man has saved the Quantum Realm,
after the Vibranium is secured by Wakanda
and the Guardians of the Galaxy protect the universe again,
the Russo brothers return to the silver screen
with their newest hero, WordWoman, disguised
as a middle-aged mother and wife.
She wields a pen. A journal. A library of slender books.
No one would ever suspect she could be a hero,
least of all her. Heck, she can't even keep the rodents
out of her garden, much less root the evil out of the world.
Audiences yawn as they watch her sit at her kitchen counter
in her slouchy sweater and wool slippers. For hours.
"Where's the action?" someone shouts as he gets up
for another bucket of buttered popcorn.
That's when Stan Lee shows up as the UPS man,
shocking everyone, and he delivers her a copy
of Rilke's *Letters to a Young Poet*. Cut to the next scene,
she's in a black pleather bodysuit wearing lots of mascara,
a dark ponytail high on her head streaked with silver.
She's ripped and ready to do what it takes to make peace.
"Was that Neruda?" someone whispers in the front aisle
as she slings poems, one after another,
stunning her enemies into silence.
"I think Amichai," someone says. "Or Shihab Nye."
When the movie is over, most people are grumbling
that superheroes just aren't what they used to be.
But in the back, a young girl is scribbling
words on a napkin. She's ready to save the world.

GETTING CLOSE

In the photo he is dancing,
his arms a strong diagonal,
his tie flying forward
even as he comes to a still point,
balanced for a moment
on the toes of his tap shoes,
his body a lightning bolt
in a crisp white shirt.
I focus on his face,
see the will it takes
to make his body stop in time,
see his easy smile,
the invitation in his eyes,
a blend of pride and play.
I lean in until his face is a blur,
as if by coming closer,
I might feel the breath
that isn't there, breathe in
the warmth of his being.
I love entering
this photo sometimes,
or more rightly,
love the way this photo
enters me until
I ring with the truth
of how it is to love
this boy who did not
become a man,
this boy who chose
to make his body
stop in time,
this lightning bolt
captured on film,
unpredictable, powerful,
something no one
could hold forever,
this love that strikes me
every time I think of him,
I still feel it, the charge.

SEROTINOUS

Even the word *surrender*
suggests some agency,
but perhaps
what is asked of us
is zero. Perhaps
we are like the seed
of the lodgepole pine
that opens through
no effort of its own.
It needs the heat
of a wildfire blaze.
Then the seed is released
into the very blackened,
desolate world
that seemed hellbent
on destroying it,
but it is the carbon-rich
soil left by the fire
that feeds the seed
and helps the tree grow.
No surrender.
No effort.
Who could ask
for the fire?
The seed did not.
It did nothing at all.
And now, the pine,
how green, how tall.

How the World Goes On

The burr relies on brittle prickers,
cheat grass on sharp and spiky barbs,
and then there's the milkweed
that attaches its seeds to gossamer fluff
and spills forth in an ecstasy of diaphanous floss,
white puffs of wish-downy, dream-gauzy,
breeze-easy lushness. Oh, heart,
this, too, is what survival looks like—
an almost impossible softness
that gathers light in silky froth
and entrusts itself to the wind.

SOMEWHERE IN THE UNIVERSE

There is this hour when my mother
and daughter and I are side by side
shaping soft red dough into tiny balls
to add to the green spritz wreaths;
the kitchen smells of almond
and butter, and there are carols
on the stereo and it's going to snow.
Yes, I know there are thousands
of imperfect moments,
but there is also this moment
when I find myself smiling
in a small kitchen in a narrow river valley
in a vast mountain range on a large continent
on a smallish planet in one galaxy among
the hundreds of billions that somehow
all belong to a universe that's expanding faster
than we think it should—
and as I hum along to a medieval hymn
about how a rose is blooming,
my heart scoured, my heart full,
how is it I, too, am a chord unfolding from minor
to major *amid the cold of winter?*
How is it I am a rose blooming bright,
faster than I think I should,
this dark season strangely blessed?

LIKE THE PEONY

Like the peony that opens
and opens and opens,
this is how I want to meet life:
surviving the cold,
then returning to bloom
again. And again.
That vibrant. That many-petaled.
Embarrassingly fulsome,
as if life just can't
get enough of itself.
Truth is, life cuts you to the ground
and you lose all but the roots.
Sometime you lose those, too.
How is it, then, comes
the chance to bloom again,
to be less master of life
and more servant to
what pushes through?
I want to be fluent in blooming.
I want to trust the possibility
of sweet spring perfume
as much as I trust
the inevitability of frost.
I am so grateful for beauty,
albeit brief,
for the chance to be naked,
tender, soft.

Because

So I can't save the world—
can't save even myself,
can't wrap my arms around
every frightened child, can't
foster peace among nations,
can't bring love to all who
feel unlovable.
So I practice opening my heart
right here in this room and being gentle
with my insufficiency. I practice
walking down the street heart first.
And if it is insufficient to share love,
I will practice loving anyway.
I want to converse about truth,
about trust. I want to invite compassion
into every interaction.
One willing heart can't stop a war.
One willing heart can't feed all the hungry.
And sometimes, daunted by a task too big,
I ask myself, *What's the use of trying?*
But today, the invitation is clear:
to be ridiculously courageous in love.
To open the heart like a lilac in May,
knowing freeze is possible
and opening anyway.
To take love seriously.
To give love wildly.
To race up to the world
as if I were a puppy,
adoring and unjaded,
stumbling on my own exuberance.
To feel the shock of indifference,
of anger, of cruelty, of fear,
and stay open. To love as if it matters,
as if the world depends on it.

In Crepuscular Light

These warm summer evenings
I take in the nighthawks
looping above the field.
I take in their fast and agile flight,
take in their long and pointed wings.
Come winter, I will be grateful
to have stored such things.
When the nighthawks are gone
and the world is dim,
I will want to remember them—
their aerialist displays, the way
they make of the dusk a playground,
the way the whole night
seems to hang on an angling wing.
Oh, summer is such a generous thing.
Even the dark is charged with the thrill
of living. Even this heart, wounded
and bruised, can't help but open
to the wheeling of nighthawks,
how they arc and sweep
as the sun disappears
and then continue their swooping
long after the light is gone.

Settling In

The way old friends walk together—
that is how it is today with me and grief.
We stop and admire the cloudless sky,
the flight of a hawk. We keep walking.
There isn't much to say, so we're quiet.
No bluster. No drama. No striving.
Sometimes we catch a glimpse
of our shadows and wave.
It's not uphill, we're not out of breath.
I didn't know walking with grief
could be like this.
There was a time, I remember, before.
Now, I can't imagine not feeling close.
When the walk is done,
there's no need to say goodbye.
I hold out my hand. We go on.

THE CONVERSATION

Outside the kitchen door,
your large green crocs sit, empty.

I slip my feet into them
and shuffle around the porch.

Life went on, I say to the air, to you.
I scuffle past the cinquefoil

with its plentiful yellow blooms,
shamble past the small and robust lilac bush

friends gave us after you died.
Look at all this life, I say to you,

to the air. *It's in everything.*
It's in me, too, this burgeoning.

And then I'm crying with the all of it—
the fierce sun and the blur of hummingbirds

and the ache in my chest and
the green in the field and

the terrible, wondrous truth—
Life goes on. For a long time,

I shuffle and talk to the air.
As always, your silence speaks back.

I listen to it beneath the rush
of the river, beneath the riot of birds,

beneath the shush of the wind
weaving through the grass.

THE CHOOSING

Perhaps I no longer believe in happiness
as the goal. Not that I am against happiness,
but being in this very uncomfortable moment
with little light and a vicious chill, my arms wrapped
around my growing girl, both our hearts breaking
from sorrow and fear, both of us too well aware
of what can be lost, well, I would not trade this moment
for any wide-grinned hour of beach and sun,
wouldn't rather be anywhere else with anyone—
I would choose again and again to be here
on the dark sidewalk with my girl in my arms,
our hearts so raw, the space between us so warm.

WITH ASTONISHING TENDERNESS

When, in the middle of the night,
you wake with the certainty you've
done it all wrong, when you wake
and see clearly all the places you've failed,
in that moment, when dreams will not return,
this is the chance for your most gentle voice—
the one you reserve for those you love most—
to say to you quietly, *oh sweetheart,*
this is not yet the end of the story.
Sleep will not come, but somehow,
in that wide-awake moment there is peace—
the kind that does not need
everything to be right before it arrives.
The kind that comes from not fighting
what is real. The peace that rises
in the dark on its sure dark wings
and flies true with no moon, no stars.

Gleaning

—with thanks to Erika Moss

She arrived with a dozen pears
she had gleaned from an orchard.
I place them in a scalloped dish
and sniff the naked air,
hungry for the scent of pear.
I think of gleaning,
the wisdom in gathering
what has been left behind,
how now I glean memories
that at first were passed over
in favor of others that were sweeter,
or bigger, or more perfectly formed.
But now it's these smaller, harder
memories that sustain me.
I love walking the rows of the mind
to find there are memories still hanging.
I gather them into the bowl of my heart
where they will ripen
in their own time.
Almost forgotten,
they are even more sweet.

The medicine of surrender

comes with no spoonful of sugar.
No promises, no back-up plans,
no returns, no insurance.
The medicine of surrender
never tastes the way you expect,
never tastes the same next time,
seldom has the hoped-for effect.
And if there is some part of you
that thinks it might not be affected,
that thinks it might hold back,
that part is most likely the first part
to be flooded with the relentless
truth of what is. Oh surrender!
The surest medicine that exists.
There are infinite side effects.
Wonder. Freedom. Rawness.
It's like opening the dictionary
to the word *heaven*. Or *obliteration*.
And knowing it's the same thing.
It's like playing spin the bottle with life,
and you French kiss whatever you get.
It's the only remedy that can help you
be whole. The only real medicine there is.

ALL AT ONCE

Before I woke, my son and I
were eating breakfast—

a beautiful brown-crusted boule,
warm from the oven,

and he was slicing it and making
a giant mess of it,

the bread tearing and smushing,
and we were laughing—

his head was thrown back
with the joy of making a mess,

carefree and goofy and foolish.
Crumbs everywhere.

God, how I loved him
as he smashed a hardboiled egg

onto the uneven slice.
How I loved him

as he stuffed his mouth
with the botched bread and egg.

How I loved him as we laughed
and laughed and laughed.

How I loved him when I woke
and he was dead,

his absence making the love
no less beautiful, no less true,

our laughter no less mirthful
in the empty room.

AFTER I TOLD THEM ABOUT OUR TWO DAUGHTERS, THEY ASKED IF WE HAD MORE CHILDREN

There's no easy way to say it.
I told them. *Our son died.*
They were sitting across
from us, our new neighbors,
afternoon sun streaming
into the room with low spring gold.
Their grandson sat on our floor,
a teaspoon the only toy I had for him.
He mouthed it with quiet joy.
Was it an accident? she asked.
He chose to take his own life, I said.
The words hung in the air
like dust that sparkles—
then seems to disappear.
What I did not say:
Once we sat on this couch
and read books, watched *Peter Pan*,
built pirate forts with pillows, searched
for Waldo and snuggled when it rained.
Once he, too, chewed on my teaspoons
before he built computers and
took AP Statistics and helped me buy a Ford.
They murmured, *I'm sorry,*
because that's what people say
when there is nothing else to say.
When the talk soon turned
to bonfires and building permits,
I did not mind. It was enough
to have acknowledged he was here.
What I did not say, but somehow said:
Just because he's dead
doesn't mean he's gone.
We have three children—
two daughters and a son.

PERSPECTIVE

And the mountains rose
and eroded completely
and the great sea flooded all
and the great sea left and
the great sea flooded and left again
and the land was forced up,
and then pulled from both sides
until the center broke
and slid down to create a great rift
and the volcanoes spewed lava
and the ash covered all
and the glaciers scrubbed
and the rocks avalanched
and the earth slumped
and today I sit in the valley
and stare at the mountain
with a dusting of white
on its wide shoulders
light gathering in its clefts
and I think, my god,
isn't it peaceful?

LETTER TO VINCENT ABOUT THAT AFTERNOON

Would you have painted me then,
in that moment when my hands
were red with the blood of my son
as I knelt on the dark wood floor?
Is there a red pigment sacred enough
for that scene?
Would you have drawn the hunch
in my back, the bend in my knees,
or would you have focused your frame
on the stretch of my fingers
as I moved them through the spill?
I would not have wanted your eyes there,
but would you have seen the devotion?
Is that something canvas can hold?
Could you, through brush stroke and shade,
have found the beauty in this moment,
this most broken moment, this moment
of ravaged hope, this most honest
moment in my life, this moment
when for the last time I touched him?

NOT OVERHEARD IN THE PARKING LOT

How are you?
she asks walking by
as I sit on my bumper
and unlace my ski boots.
And I say, *The track*
is amazing today,
and it's true,
the snow is hard and fast
and my lungs are still burning
from pushing myself
in the cold winter air.
What I mean is, *I miss*
my son every minute,
and my heart feels like
a skinned rabbit still alive.
She says, *What length*
are your skis?
I know what she means is,
Oh friend, I have felt that way, too.
And I tell her *One ninety,*
and we talk about how much
has changed over the years—
like ski lengths,
like skins versus scales.
What I mean:
Like the way a person is here
and then they are not.
Like the way I once
could hold him.
Like the way
he could once hold me.

It Was Impossible Until It Wasn't

It was like an ice floe in December
when the river builds up a dam of ice
and then backs up,
and the pressure builds
until the river is powerful enough
to break the dam down.
This is how it was when,
sitting beside my husband in the car
and longing for closeness,
I felt it, my inner river churning
against the wall between us,
and I realized I'd created it
with my own coldness—
and then came the rush of warm tears
and the gush of a desperate *I'm sorry*.
And in an instant
the dam broke
and the car was bank-full
with thick currents of laughter
and I was so grateful
for the one brave second
when the heart knew the truth—
how we move forward
when we see how we've made
obstacles of ourselves
and then use everything we've got
to bring our walls down.

BECOMING THE BIRD

Once on a bridge
I had met a hope,
a radiant maybe,
a glint of perhaps,
but I am so far
from that glint today
that when I stand
again on that bridge
I almost hate hope
with its stupid wings,
always promising
to carry us toward
something better.
I stand on that bridge
and stand on that bridge,
my inner perch
empty, silent.
I turn to face
the autumn wind.
It batters my bare skin.
I sing full-throat into the gale.

THAT TIME

It was like driving through a winter storm
　for years, day after week after month
　　after night after morning of white-knuckled,
　stiff-shouldered worry. No tracks to follow,
no sign of a centerline, no rails on the edge,
　and where are the snowplows, and what
　　good is a map when you can't read the signs?
　　　There were whole months of whiteout, driving snow-blind
　and slow, whole seasons of running the wipers on high
in an attempt to see just one inch further.
　　It was icy roads, skidding with the baby in back.
　　　It was wishing I could ask someone else
　　to take the wheel. It was frozen-slick and slippery
　with no studded snow tires. It was sliding with no brakes.
　It was what I woke to every day
and what I dreamed at night.
　If there was beauty, I was often too afraid to see it.
I wish I could tell you I was brave.
　It was slow to change,
　　like a spring that arrives only to leave again.
　　One day the drifts were gone and the roads
　　　were dry and the sky was wide blue and clear.
　　　But it wasn't like snow, was it?
　　Some things don't just melt away.
　Some storms transform the landscape.
　Some storms transform the driver.

THE PRAYERS

When I asked the world to open me,
I did not know the price.
When I wrote that two-word prayer in the sand,
I did not know loss was the key,
devastation the hinge,
trust was the dissolution
of the idea of a door.
When I asked the world to open me,
I could never have said *Yes* to what came next.
Perhaps I imagined the waves
knew only how to carry me.
I did not imagine they would also pull me under.
When I asked the world to open me,
I had not imagined drowning
was the way to reach the shore.
The waves of sorrow dragged me down
with their tides of unthinkable loss.
The currents emptied my pockets
and stripped me of my ideas.
I was rolled and eroded
and washed up on the sand
like driftwood—softened.
I sprawled there and wept,
astonished to still be alive.
It is not easy to continue to pray this way.
Open me.
And yet it is the truest prayer I know.
The other truest prayer,
though sometimes I long
to reject its truth, is *Thank you.*

AMAZING GRACE

At what point in the avalanche
do we realize there's nothing
to be done but be pummeled
and tumbled and broken
by the world?
At what point do we know
that no matter how hard we swim,
the current will carry
us over the falls
to the rocks below?
At what point are we sure
we can't save our beloveds,
not from the world and not
from themselves?
In that moment,
and perhaps only then,
grace comes in to do
what the will cannot,
and whatever it is
that is larger than us
makes a home in us—
like fitting the whole sky
into our hand, then
opening that hand
to pray.

III

SAMUNION

————

n. praise inspired by connection with others, the world,
the divine, and the many parts of ourselves; a sense of being in cooperation
with the whole;
the elation that arises when we trust everything belongs
and transforms together—even people, things and
circumstances we dislike or resist—and we are in service
to that belonging and transformation

from the Proto-Indo-European root *sam-* (to sing) + *union,* pronounced [*suh-*
myoon-y*uhn*] (rhymes with *communion*)

The Grand Quilt

I don't believe we can stitch together
only scraps of beauty, squares of light.
I don't believe in a quilt that doesn't also
have patches of sorrow, blocks of ache.
Such pieces are, of course, much harder
to want to stitch in. But it matters
that we do not exclude them.
It matters right now that we don't pretend
they do not exist.
It matters that we sew every piece
into the grand cloth.
It matters, too,
how we sew these pieces in,
perhaps using our finest silk thread,
perhaps with an elaborate stitch
our grandmother taught us,
or perhaps we must use
a stitch we make up
because no one ever taught us
how to do this most difficult task—
to meet what at first seems unwanted, wrong,
and to incorporate it into the whole
and to do this for as long as we can stitch,
that's how long.

THE LONG MARRIAGE

Perhaps I know you best in the dark—
that nightly shrine
where my belly meets your spine,
where the bend of my knees
meets the bend of your knees,
where my warmth meets your warmth,
the night a vase
in which we place
the stems of our bodies,
in which we flower
through touch.
And nothing must be said
and nothing must be done
except to meet the long familiar nakedness.

Perhaps I know you best in the dark—
these lightless hours when
we sit in the midst of brokenness
and my hand finds your hand,
and my silence finds your silence,
my loss, your loss,
and together, somehow,
we find an impossible calm.
And nothing must be said.
And nothing can be done to change the past.
We meet in the these darkened hours
with nothing but our willingness
to meet these darkened hours,
these hours we would have pushed away,
these hours that grow us inside each other.

In Times of Great Darkness

I want to do for you
what the sun does for me:
coax you to come
outside, to breathe in
the golden air.
I want to warm you
and enter you,
fill you with brilliance,
make your muscles melt,
make your mind shush.
I want to prepare for you
luminous paths
that span across deep space,
thaw any part of you
that feels frozen,
find any cracks
and slip shine into them.
I want to intensify
your shadow
so you might better know
your own shape.
I want to encourage you
to open, wider, wider,
want to teach you
to write your own name
in light.

NEW TERRITORY

My grief has inside it a forest, thriving,
evergreens of all ages, each tree grown
from a seed of gratitude, each seed

sown from a kindness, a beauty,
a caring word. Some trees were planted
by strangers, others by beloveds,

and others I planted myself.
See how it is that in these moments
when I think my feet are too leaden

to take another step, the sunlight
will sift through the overstory
and shine a path. Sometimes

the whole walk is just one step,
but one step is all it takes to not
be stuck. There are glades where

song gathers and I can rest,
trees where I can climb and find a nest
made of thankfulness large enough

to hold me. I didn't know
how vast the forest was until
I knew how wide grief could be.

And so I keep planting trees.
I am learning to trust the shade,
to breathe in more deeply

the fragrant air, and despite grief,
because of grief, I am learning to walk
deeper in, then deeper still.

Never the Same

Sometimes a person wakes
believing they are a storm.
It's hard to deny it, what
with all the rain pouring out
of the gutters of the mind,
all the gusts blowing through,
all the squalls, all the gray.
But by afternoon, it seems obvious
they are a garden about to sprout.
By night, it's clear they are a moon—
luminous, radiant, faithful.
That's the danger, I suppose,
of believing any frame.
Let me believe, then, in curiosity,
in wonder, in change.
Let me trust how essential it is
to stumble into the trough
of the unknown, marvel how
trough becomes wings becomes
faith becomes dawn. Let me trust
uncertainty is a sacred path.

After the Undressing

I had thought I was already naked.
I had thought I had shed
the mask, the robe, the dress,
the flimsy garments that tease.
I thought I had nothing left
to remove. Then came
slipping out of my laugh.
Taking off my smile.
Dropping my role, my hope.
Losing what I thought I knew.
I could never have said yes to this.
It happened anyway.
I am less myself, only more.
There is a shawl of compassion, though—
its threads made of sunrise gold.
This. Whoever does the undressing
wraps me now in this.

Falling in Love with Life on the Equinox

Because after the sunshine
slipped under my sweater,
snowflakes teased my cheek.
Because this morning's silence
became mid-morning geese.
Because waking. Because sleep.
Because after the memorial
for a beloved and wizened man
we watched kids walk across
the stage at school. Because
foolishness. Because truth.
Because buds swell on willows
and still the garden sits untouched.
Because love. Because fear.
Because my heart is here and
not here. Because there are moments
we feel ourselves balanced
between two sides of the same life.
Because balance lasts only a moment.
Because day. Because night.

THE ONE WHO THRIVES

for my daughter, a year later

She has learned to bloom
like the tuberose,
opening in the light
but becoming more potent
in the dark.
Sweet scent of honey.
Tenacious scent of jasmine.
The hard-won scent
of hope.
Scent of the one
who has learned to thrive
when thriving
doesn't feel possible.
Scent of resilience.
Scent of *I can*.
Scent of the one
who finds grace
on the inside.
Scent of elusive beauty.
Scent of the one
who meets the soils
made of sorrow,
who brings to the world
a gift as astonishing
as a night-blooming flower,
a gift as honest
as the moon.

I Didn't Think I Could Do It

But I found myself
rigid in the room where my son
took his life. And I sat
on the floor in the doorway
where he had last sat,
where his blood had pooled
and the air had briefly smelled
of burning. I sat there
beneath the wall
where the bullet had made
its narrow hole. I sat there
with my coil of sorrow.
I didn't want to meet it.
I desperately wanted to meet it.
I wanted to give sorrow space.
I wanted to crawl inside it.
I wanted to be anywhere
but there on the dark wood floor
in the night-dark room,
and I wanted to be wholly,
completely, obliteratingly there.
Fear-ridden, ferocious, I met it all,
felt the current pushing through.
Acceptance is a filament
that takes our resistance
and makes it bright,
makes it luminous enough
that we might see ourselves
exactly as we are.
I did not find my son
in that doorway. Perhaps
I had hoped I would.
But I saw the light
that came with me.
I softened into that light.

SELF-COMPASSION

It's like the scent of rain
after a month of drought,
the way it rises up and fills the lungs,
quiets the body
and gentles the mind—

that's what it's like
when, after grasping
and spinning and reaching
and clenching, at last,
exhausted with my own fear,

I lay my hand on my own heart
and see through my thoughts
and practice loving
what is beneath my palm:
this frightened woman

and the life that lives through her.
Not a single promise I will be safe,
but when I press my open hand
into the beat of my anxious heart
what was dry becomes loamy,

what was cracked becomes rich,
and a faint sweetness
tendrils through me like incense,
soothing as a lullaby
that opens in the dark.

BIOLUMINESCENCE

Sometimes, when I fear
the small light I bring
isn't big enough or bright
enough, I think of that night
on the beach years ago
when every step I took
in the cool wet sand turned
a glowing, iridescent blue—
and the waves themselves
were a flashing greenish hue—
imagine we could do
what 7.9 billion
one-celled plankton can do—
can shine when it's dark,
can shine when agitated,
can shine with our own
inner light and trust when we all
bring the tiny light we have
it's enough to illumine the next step
in the long stretch of night.

LUMBRICUS TERRESTRIS

On a day when the world is weighty,
  dark and dense with need,
    I want to be the earthworm
      that gives itself over to tunneling,
its every movement an act
  of bringing spaciousness.
    And when minutes feel crushed by urgency,
I want to meet the world wormlike,
  which is to say grounded,
    consistent, even slow.
No matter how desperate the situation,
  the worm does not tunnel faster
    nor burrow more.
It knows it can take decades
  to build fine soil.
    To whatever is compacted,
the worm offers its good worm work,
  quietly bringing porosity
    to what is trodden, compressed.
So often, in my rush to repair,
  I end up exhausted.
Let my gift to the world be
 my constancy, a devotion to openness,
    my willingness to be with what is.
      Let my gift to myself be patience
as I tend what is dense and dark.

A Closer Look

I recall how dad gave me glass vials
and encouraged me to go to the lake, take samples,
then bring them back to the house
where he'd taught me to use a glass dropper
to put a small bead between slide and slip,
then focus the microscope
to spy on all the life pulsing there:
thin oblong shapes and zooming dots,
spinning green circles and segmented strands—
it was like eavesdropping on adult conversation,
like being given the key to enter life itself,
and I, an eager traveler into invisible realms,
spent hours staring into that intricate world.
Memory is sometimes a chance to meet
a drop of the past, then wonder about the world
beyond what we first see. I thought this
was a memory about lake water, glass slides,
a microscope. I look closer. I see trust.
Pulsing love. A father teaching curiosity.

PRESERVING SWEETNESS

The whole house smelled
of ripening then, the day mom
made apples into sauce.
The heat from the stove
made the small kitchen
swelter, and the autumn air
almost shone with the bright
scent of Jonathan, Pippin,
Winesap, Cortland.
Her arms were strong then,
straining to push the blushing
pink mash through the sieve,
slow and stiff with the effort.
Perhaps there is a language
somewhere that has a word
for this: the way something sweet
can linger, how it flows over,
around and through the body
like the cidery scent of apples
till it lodges itself in the memory.
Oh Mama, I want to serve this
sweetness to you now,
the memory of you stirring
with two good, strong arms,
the way you put all of who you were
into the smallest of acts,
how fifty years later,
what you did that one afternoon
still matters.

Though I Knew Love Before

Not until my world dissolved
in an instant did I begin to understand
the communion of hearts.

Not until I could not put one minute
in front of the next did I begin
to understand infinite devotion.

Not until I lost my own flesh did I begin
to understand the muscle of spirit.
I will never love the loss, never,

but I love the life that rushes in after.
I love the intimacy
of those who have lost—

how we find each other and offer
our open embrace, our unwalled affection,
our wildest wishes for peace.

Not until I was consumed
by the great wave of love
did I know not to fear

the great wave of love.
Only then did I learn the beauty
of ceding the self to something much greater.

Only then did I learn how love
not only carries us,
it transforms who we are forever.

Think Small

Even the smallest strand of saffron
goldens the rice and lends
its good and earthy bitterness
to each of the ten thousand
grains in the pot.

My friend says she wants
to make a bigger difference,
doubts the effect she has.
There are many ways, I think,
to reach many.

One is to do as the saffron crocus does—
put everything you have
into just a few threads,
then trust they're potent enough
to change everything.

IV

PANGLORIA

---

n. praise that arises out of an ecstatic gratefulness for life
and the ways we are intimately bonded with all;
a strange certainty that there are opportunities for praise everywhere,
even where we would rather not look

from Greek *pan-* (all) + *glory*, pronounced [pan-**glohr**-ee-*uh*]

Self-Portrait as Wetlands

After years, grief now grows in me
as honestly as sedges flourish
at the edges of the marsh.
As necessary and benign
as fresh water. As generous
as the incense of rain.
I would not wish grief away
any more than I would
wish away the blue heron,
which is to say I now see
grief as an essential part of my biome,
how without it, other parts of me
would perish. How vital
to be saturated by tears,
to not resist the floods of loss.
Grief nourishes what is here,
the self ever unfinished,
life still looking for its shape.

OF TENDERNESS

So easily the thin rind
pulls away from the clementine
to reveal what is tender,
what is sweet.

It matters, I think,
the way we offer
ourselves to each other.

I think of how it falls open,
the peel of the clementine.

I think of how sometimes,
when I ask how you are,
you, too, fall open
and give me everything.

What a gift
when I don't need to pry.
What a gift, the bright scent
of conversation,
how the tang of it
lingers in the air.

I long to open
for you this way, too.
Trust begins here.

Saving Grace

I didn't even see
the slender red salamander
curled in the middle
of the country road,
but Brad stopped to kneel
beside it and told us
if you pick them up
by the tail, they will lose
their tail—an attempt
to distract a predator
while the rest
of the body escapes.
So tenderly, he brushed
the small amphibian
into his open palm,
then gently placed it intact
in the wet grass beside the road.
If this day were a novel,
I'd say the morning walk
was foreshadowing.
Everywhere we went that day
there were hands
that opened in kindness—
to greet, to serve cake,
to hug, to wave—
as if everyone agreed it matters,
the way we treat each other.
How quickly we can fall apart
when threatened.
How easily, sometimes,
we are saved.

IN THOSE QUIET HOURS

For two weeks after he died,
I'd fall asleep exhausted
only to wake just past midnight.
Desperate, I'd claw at sleep,
frantic to catch it and clutch it,
but always it slipped my grasp
and I'd lie awake till morning.

My friend suggested
I reframe those sleepless hours
as a sacred time, an intimate,
personal quiet time. Not as a problem.
Not as something to be treated.
Not something to be feared.
That night, as I emerged from sleep,
dreams dripping from me like water,
I did not resist the waking.
Instead, eyes closed, heart open,
still lying in bed, I said,
I love you, Finn. I miss you, sweetheart.
And woke on the shore of morning.
Ever since, it happens just like this—
when I slip from sleep,
I tell my son I love him
and slide unknowingly
back into the tide of dreams.

How many hundreds of times,
when he was young, did I go to him
when he cried out in the night?
I'd press my palms against his chest
until his breath was a skiff for dreams.

Years later, though I can't feel his hands,
though I don't hear the lullaby of his breath,
somehow he arrives to comfort me.
And though I don't hear him say
the words I'd always say to him,
I feel them float above me like a blanket,
warm in the cool night air—
Shhh. I'm here. It's okay. I'm here.

DACTYLOGRAPHY

Just when you think you know who you are,
you take a closer look at your heart
and notice it is marked
with the whorls and loops and arches
of everyone you've ever loved
and everyone who has ever loved you—
those who left you, who broke you,
and those who still charm and nourish you.
As if the heart's reason for being
is simply to be shaped and reshaped
by the hands of the world.
As if the detectives of love
could visit your heart
with their fingerprint powder
and lifting tape and unfold the mystery
of how you became who you are,
fashioned by the uniqueness of others,
discovering your heart
is not a crime scene at all,
but a rare and incomparable work of art.

WORDLESSLY

With such gentleness,
he stood behind me
and held me as I wept,
held me the way a pond holds a lotus,
the way a scarf holds perfume,
the way a man who has lost his child
holds the mother of their child,
his hands so light on my hands
as our fingers laced into a tender weave,
held me the way the pericardium holds the heart,
the way the eye holds a tear
then lets it slip away.

Memory, Like a Passport

That winter night you streaked
down the walkway in your undies
and jumped into the snowbank,
I think of it now,
your raucous laughter,
your feral joy
as you emerged frosty and grinning;
I think of how you wore your elation
on the outside,
not hidden up a sleeve,
not tucked in a pocket
where no one could see.
It didn't save you, your wild joy—
perhaps that's not what joy is for—
but some nights it saves me.
I still smell the clean sharp cold of it,
hear the glee-giddy,
mirth-ringing choruses of it
like an anthem to a country
that has changed its borders
and still, somehow, lets me in.

ONE BOY

Today the heart is full of ghosts—
one doing backflips and one
eating ice cream and one throwing
rocks in the river. One drops
a camera into a lily pond while trying
to take a picture. One peels apples
and one rides on my hip and one
sings country songs. One lights a candle
and one blows it out and one spends hours
arguing about which of the ghosts is most right.
And one is never satisfied. And one
has a thousand dull gray eyes. And one,
one whispers, *I've got this, Mom.*
And I turn to them all, one at a time,
and say, *Welcome, you're all welcome here.*
Even the ghost who slams the door.
Even the ghost who bristles, who swears.
Ghost playing drums. Ghost aiming
nerf guns. Ghost wearing button-down shirts.
Ghost with a brain made for zeros and ones.
Ghost with hands in the dirt.
And the heart expands to hold them all—
or were its corridors already stretched?
Straight-A ghost. Red canoe ghost. Ghost
of the man I'll never know. Ghost
who sits beside me at the table,
who says nothing, sipping sweet tea.
Ghost who tucks me into bed
then slips into my dreams.

I LIVE FOR THIS MOMENT,

when my daughter stumbles
sleepy-eyed from her room
and no matter what I'm doing,
I stop and move to the corner
of the couch so she can settle
her whole weight on me.
Maybe we speak of dreams.
Maybe we converse with the cat.
Maybe we plan the day.
Maybe we say nothing at all.
All that matters is that
she is close and I nuzzle my face
into her hair and wrap an arm
around her chest and know
this is the beginning of everything,
the seed, the cosmic swirl,
the headline that's yet to be written.
To foster one moment of trust
and love is to belong
to a crucial revolution.
So vital, how we hold each other.
What happens everywhere
starts right here.

Love, Like Water

We could say the pain
was a block so great
   it could not be moved.
We could say love
did not try to move it.
   Love simply surrounded the mass
and dissolved it
the way water meets a block of salt,
   breaking apart each ionic bond
until every atom of sodium and chloride
is surrounded by molecules of water.
   And in this way,
and sooner than you'd think,
the pain was rearranged
   into minuscule bits,
and there was no part of the pain
that was not touched by love.
   The pain was no less, it's true.
But mixed with love, dispersed,
the pain became something new.
   Something vital that encouraged
a different kind of life,
a substance that supported buoyancy,
   an essential medium to carry me.

Before the Wings Appear

Snuggle, she said,
a two-syllable passport
to another world—
the world in which
she is more dream
than mask, more breath
than task, her softness
inviting my softness,
and I slipped beside
her dream-scented body
and curled myself
into her shape,
one arm draped
across her weight,
and matched my inhale
to her inhale, matched
my every exhale to hers
and listened as once again
sleep took her,
and in that moment
she was not curious,
not smart, not funny,
not brave, but so deeply
herself, and of course
I deliquesced into love,
a pilgrim in this realm
of sweet defenselessness,
the silken swirl of our breaths
weaving around us
as if the air itself knew
we were too raw,
too filled with transformation
not to have
a cocoon.

At the Market

Now when I walk through the market
I think of how someone else here
beside the stir-fry cart and the tie-dye tent
has just lost a beloved
and is hiding tears behind sunglasses.
Not knowing who they are,
I try to treat everyone with kindness.
Meanwhile the day is beautiful
for everyone, no matter how whole,
how broken our hearts. It gathers us all
in a grand blue embrace.
I stroll through the gift of a Friday
morning surrounded by arugula
and strawberries, muffins, lilies,
and all these other fragile hearts,
all of us saying *Excuse me, Good morning,*
How are you, It's nice to see you today.

MEADOW

Walking through tall grass
on a narrow path, my fingers
spread wide to pull through the seedheads.
As if to touch is to be touched.
As if, with open palms,
I could pull this beauty
inside me and carry it with me
until I give it to you—
as if I could somehow
slip a whole meadow into your pocket
so you could unfold it anytime
and wander through grass
as high as your chest
and feel how the vastness
reminds us who we are.

When it looks as if I am talking to myself

I'm talking to the dead.
Oh, look at the bunny,
I say to the empty kitchen.
I didn't know I would be
the kind of woman
who talks to the dead,
who narrates the day,
who believes they hear me
after midnight when I whisper
I miss you.
I say *I love you*
as I walk in the spruce
and falling snow,
say *Isn't it beautiful*
into the crystalline air,
and the scene is more beautiful
for the sharing.
When I am alone,
I am always talking to the dead
about what it's like to be here
in their absence.
How strangely wondrous
life can be after a loss.
I feel their presence
in the listening,
feel how the listening wraps
its tender arms around me,
feel how gently the listening
leans in to cradle my face
with silence.

APRICITY

The miracle is not to walk on water.
The miracle is to walk on the green Earth
in the present moment, to appreciate
the peace and beauty that are available now.
—Thich Nhat Hanh

Today the miracle is to sit
in the sunlit room and be
in the sunlit room,
to be here and only here,
here in the bountiful silence,
here in the shifting shadows,
here in the hands of midwinter,
not in this same room five years ago,
but now as the tulips
drop the soft curls of their petals
like lingering pink praise.
So seldom in these grief-ridden days
do I feel a feeling as pure
as this peace that arrives
on the low-angled light
when I am quiet and still
and the world invites me
to show up for whatever
slim warmth there is,
and know this is enough.

No Longer Empty-Handed

—after the poet pointed out there are dozens of
well-known euphemisms for male masturbation
and none for women's

How could I not start to think
of circling the black hole,
polishing the pearl,
rubbing the rose bud,
loosening the tight knot,
spreading the soft butter,
frosting the sweet cake,
dancing on the vortex,
getting sucked into the eddy,
diving into the deep end,
stirring the soup till it's hot.
What does it mean
we don't have language
for a woman who pleases herself?
Consider the tectonic shift,
the one-handed time warp,
churning the cream,
climbing pink mountain,
traveling to the tiny temple,
spinning in dark silk.
Others are choking chickens,
spanking monkeys,
beating meat,
wanking,
but let's call this what it is:
swirling the universe,
mining for diamonds,
finding hidden treasure,
wishing, wishing, wishing for a genie,
the reason I can't answer the phone.

After the Memorial

The mother walked
in a deep river gorge
forged by water and time.
She knew herself alone.
She moved with no urgency.
She stepped as if she'd forgotten
what time was.
She paused at the wild currants
and pulled the small red fruits
into her mouth.
She paused on the bridge
and watched the water
continue its forging.
She paused on a flat rock,
removed her shoes
and slipped her feet
into the cold water.
She did not mind
the hem of her black dress
spilled into the stream.
She sat.
She didn't weep until she did.
Then she wept until she didn't.
She sat until she forgot
she was sitting.
She sat until
there was a clearing in her,
the way the river will eventually clear
after it's been muddied by the rain.
There's no magic number
for how many minutes
or hours or years
it takes to clear.
It is, perhaps, sufficient to know
clearing happens.
At some point, she rose
and walked toward home.
She was not alone.
There was nothing that was not beautiful.

THERE IS THIS MOMENT

with the full moon rising
and a large bird of prey
gliding spirals in the sky
and my husband on my right
my sweet friend on my left
and the two-person band
transforming sorrow into joy
just by singing it in harmony
and giving the song their everything,
and maybe that's what is ours to do—
to give ourselves wholly to a moment
as if we are the singers and life the song,
so I give myself to the low summer sun
and the dust on my feet,
to the pucker of lime
and the tears of my friend,
give myself to the ache that never leaves
and the relentless beauty that ever arrives,
and the more I give myself to the world,
the more the world rushes in
and says, *Home, home, home,*
you are home.

NOW THAT THE STAKES ARE LOW

For the fourth time in four weeks,
I slip my spade into the dark soil
of the half-circle garden.
I make twenty shallow holes,
then lift the pansies from crinkly
plastic containers and drop
the root-bound squares into the earth.
Within hours, the small brown bunny
arrives with his pink twitchy nose
and his small round lump
of soft bunny body,
and while I wash dishes
I meet through the window
his innocent, unblinking gaze
as he consumes a dozen
deep purple petals
in small, efficient tugs.
He looks at me as if to say,
You love me. And I do.
I croon at the bunny how
cute his small ears. How perfect
his bliss. How good he is
for eating his pretty bunny food.
Tomorrow, the rest
of the blooms will be gone.
In a week, the leaves will
be gone, too. Every. Single. One.
And I will go buy more pansies.
How sweet it's become,
this path of surrender,
the strange joy that rises in me
when I see my precious pansies
nibbled to the roots.
Now that the stakes are low,
it's much easier to bow
to the way things are.
For the price of pansies,
I can practice again and again
how to find real delight
in this art of letting go.

The Broken Heart Goes Dancing

—at The Infamous Stringdusters show

Give me a night made of strings,
a night that is plucked
and strummed and bowed and picked,
a night with a driving, ecstatic music
and nothing to do but be danced
by the night as if each string of dobro
and fiddle and bass is attached
to an arm, a foot, a hip,
to the curling edge of an upper lip—
and even the broken heart is tugged
from its chair by bronze-coated strings
until it's an open and rhythmic thing
that beats for the bliss of it, beats
for the song of it, beats
for the joy-swaying head-shaking lift
of it, beats because that's what a heart
is for, and for hours the night
pulls every string, and the heart
beats out *More, please, more.*

TRANSLATION

In a quiet house
a woman can have
quiet thoughts,
can sit in the quiet
and let the quiet
inside. In a quiet house,
a woman can sit
on the couch
in a quiet room
and watch the leaves
out the window
as they do not move
in the wind
that is not there.
How quiet it is,
the kind of deep quiet
that makes a woman
slip into the quiet
as if it's inevitable,
and the quiet seeps in
and fills her the way
water seeps quietly
into the sand,
and the house is quiet
and the air is quiet
and the woods are quiet
and the world is quiet
and the woman is quiet
until she rhymes
with quiet,
until she becomes
the attention
that meets the quiet
and the quiet
becomes her.

BLUSTERY

Into the wind, the whipping
wind, the fierce, tempestuous,
mighty wind, we skied
as it pushed us and
bent us and slapped us
in a language made wholly
of howl—how alive we were,
laughing into the gale,
taking the storm into our lungs,
as if our breath could learn
its syntax, translate
its tongues of gust and squall
into wild, untamable mirth.
This is how we carried the storm
home in our bloodstream.
This is how, even now,
I feel it in my lips,
an uncontrollable, reckless smile.

TODAY'S SERMON

was a single drop
of melted snow
that clung to the tip
of a tight red bud
at the end
of a naked branch.
It didn't have to
shout or sing
to make me fall in love
with the way afternoon light
gathered inside it.
Such a simple pulpit,
such humble gospel,
this radiant preacher,
this silence in which
the prayer is made
of listening.

SACRED GROUND

And if, as I now know, the closet
is sacred and the bare room
is sacred and the sidewalk
and classroom and the ER
are sacred, then I trip
into the teaching
that everywhere is sacred—
not only the church, but
the alley. Not only the mosque,
but the bench.
Not only the places in candlelight
where the air is pungent
and woody with myrrh.
I want to worship
at the shrine of everywhere,
want to know every inch
of this earth as an altar—
every walk, a pilgrimage.
Every step, a step
from holy to holy
to holy.

POSTLUDE

Why the unfolding?

A year and a day after my son took his life, I had a vision. I saw the self as a white, bowl-shaped flower—a many-petaled ranunculus—and I watched as it opened and opened and infinitely opened, reaching beyond borders, beyond atmosphere, beyond our beautiful spiral of galaxy, its petals unfolding and unfolding, a timeless, unending unfolding.

There was a moment when the green stem snapped and I worried the blossom had become too big—as if an infinite unfolding was not sustainable. Then I felt it, how completely the great bloom was held not just by a stem, but by the all that is. In that moment, in my body, I came to deeply trust both the process of unfolding and the faithfulness of the holding.

Two years later, I still feel like that flower, continuously growing and opening, and at the same time I'm still learning to trust the greater Whole to carry me, to carry us all as we continue to evolve.

It comforts me to know there is no edge to the universe, no way to accidentally go beyond. We cannot be too expansive. Continuous unfolding is the nature of the universe, an energy mirrored in the inner workings of the soul. As author Brian Swimme would say, we are "cosmological beings."

Swimme synthesized modern scientific discovery to outline eleven forces that continually create and shape our universe, our planet and human consciousness. The Unfolding follows this eleven-part framework. Section one, "Verilujah," contains Seamlessness, Centration and Allurement. Section two, "Sorrom," contains Emergence, Homeostasis and Cataclysm. Section three, "Samunion," contains Synergy, Transmutation and Transformation. And the last section, "Pangloria," contains Interrelatedness and Radiance.

I hadn't written the poems with these principles of cosmic evolution in mind, but as I explored how the poems might fit into Swimme's scaffolding, I was thrilled by the energetic thrust it created and how it allowed for the emotional intensity of this collection to unfold in an organic fashion. In the Prelude, I suggest The Unfolding is something like a song. And if grief is the basso-continuo and praise is the melody, the staff is made of the science of the universe.

If you didn't read the poems in order, I don't blame you. I seldom read poetry collections from front to back, preferring to let my attention land wherever the page opens. But if you're willing, I hope you'll start again at page one and consider the energetic journeys that inform not only the ongoing creation of our universe but also the stories of our own becoming.

A Bouquet of Long-Stemmed Gratefulnesses

Thank you to my husband, Eric, my daughter Vivian, my stepdaughter Shawnee and her husband Drew. I am so grateful for our family, the ways we support each other as we continue to unfold.

Thank you, Mom, for all the ways you taught me to play, to love, to show up.

Thank you, Finn and Dad, for giving me your love light to carry.

Thank you to my wise and gentle editor, Mark S. Burrows, who believed in this book before there was a book and who reminded me of Rilke's call to praise—"because life is, because love is, because beauty is."

Thank you to Melody Stanford Martin for the book design—what a thrill when you chose pink, Finn's favorite color, and I love those delicate, mysterious blooms unfolding and dissolving.

Thank you, Paula Lepp, for playing with language with me until we arrived at exciting, nuanced words for praise. Thank you, John Mason, for scouring your archives to help me select poems. Thank you, Kyra Kopestonsky, for reading every single poem aloud with me and puzzling over the order. Thank you, Joan Shapiro, for your fabulous keen eyes.

Thank you to Joi Sharp, my spiritual teacher, for turning me again and again and again toward what is true, for helping me long to say yes to the world as it is. And to my life coach Rebecca S. Mullen, for the encouragement, the tools, the listening, the love.

And thank you to all the companion poets and readers and friends who have buoyed me with love and encouragement. Thank you, thank you, a thousand thousand thank yous.

Endnotes

The epigraph is a poem by Rainer Maria Rilke (1875–1926), written in 1921 as a dedication the poet inscribed in a book given to Leonie Zacharias (see *Sämtliche Werke*, vol. 3 [Insel Verlag, 1976], 249). The translation is by Mark S. Burrows (©2024) and is used with permission.

"Prelude": The quote from Gregory Orr is excerpted from "Not to Make Loss Beautiful…" from *Concerning the Book that is the Body of the Beloved* (Port Townsend, WA: Copper Canyon Press, 2005).

"Prelude": The quote from Brother David Steindl-Rast, OSB, is from "Spirituality as Common Sense" from *The Quest* 3:2 (1990), 12–17.

"Prelude": *The Dictionary of Obscure Sorrows* by John Koenig is published by Simon & Schuster, 2021.

"Self-Portrait as Tuning Fork": The epigraph from Joi Sharp is from a private conversation. Joi, who has been my teacher since 2009, leads *satsang* and can be found at www.joisharp.com. She is also the one who first asked me the question asked in the Prelude, "Can you say yes to the world as it is?"

"Kalsarikännit": This blended word is possible, even claimed by Finnish media and the Institute for the Languages of Finland, though it is a recent addition to this agglutinative language. It's a blend of *kalsarit* (underwear) and *känni* (drunkenness).

"It's Like This": The epigraph can be found in "The Odds of You Being Alive Are Incredibly Small," by Dina Spector, *Business Insider* (*June 11, 2012*).

"How the Healing Happens": This poem, and dozens more, was created by starting with the phrase "Today grief is _____" I was surprised how I could fill in this blank every day, even many times a day, with a different word. It helped me to be aware how quickly grief changes. And if I put an object in the blank, any object, I was surprised how almost everything had something to teach me about grief—from pink pencil erasers to shadows to teaspoons, as in this poem.

"Somewhere in the Universe:" On Dec. 17, 2021, *National Geographic* reported that "[t]he universe is expanding faster than it should be," which is to say faster than the scientists' models predict.

"The medicine of surrender": The title came from a prompt in Mirabai Starr's online group, Holy Lament, in which she invited us to fill in the phrase "The medicine of surrender _____."

"Becoming the Bird": This poem alludes to Emily Dickinson's poem "'Hope' is the Thing with feathers"; in *The Poems of Emily Dickinson*, edited R. W. Franklin (Cambridge, MA: Belknap Press, 1999), #314.

"The Prayers:" This poem was written after listening to the incredible Kim Rosen recite "Island" by Langston Hughes, from *The Collected Poems of Langston Hughes* (Vintage Books, 1995). His poem begins with the phrase "Wave of sorrow," which finds its way into my poem. Before I wrote this poem, I danced it, listening to Kim recite "Island" to cello music played by Jami Sieber.

"The Grand Quilt": This poem is in part in response to Stuart Kestenbaum's poem "Holding the Light" in which he writes "In our imperfect world / we are meant to repair / and stitch together / what beauty there is." Published in *Only Now* (Deerbook Editions, 2013).

"Love, Like Water": My friend David Lee often says every poem should have a secret, and I want to share this poem's secret. The form with its two lines indented once, then one line indented eight times, is meant to symbolize the chemical composition of water, two hydrogens (1 proton) and one oxygen (8 protons).

"Apricity": The epigraph by Thich Nhat Hanh comes from *Touching Peace* (Parallax Press, 1992).

"Today's sermon": The title comes from a poem by the same name by Cheryl Dumesnil (*Rattle* #67, Spring 2020).

"Postlude": "The Powers of the Universe" by Brian Swimme (*EnlightenNext*, 2011).

Rosemerry Wahtola Trommer has been writing and sharing a poem a day since 2006—a practice that especially nourished her after the death of her teenage son in 2021. Her daily poems can be found on her blog, A Hundred Falling Veils, or a curated version (with optional prompts) on her daily audio series, The Poetic Path, available with the Ritual app. She is the author of *Exploring Poetry of Presence II: Prompts to Deepen Your Writing Practice*, and her poetry album, *Dark Praise*, explores "endarkenment," available anywhere you listen to music.

She also co-hosts *Emerging Form* (a podcast on creative process), *Secret Agents of Change* (a surreptitious kindness cabal), and *Soul Writer's Circle*. Her poetry has appeared on *A Prairie Home Companion*, *PBS News Hour*, *O Magazine*, *American Life in Poetry*, on Carnegie Hall stage, and on river rocks she leaves around town. Her collection *Hush* won the Halcyon Prize. *Naked for Tea* was a finalist for the Able Muse Book Award. Her most recent collections are *All the Honey* and *The Unfolding*.

In January 2024, she became the first poet laureate for Evermore, helping others through this platform to explore grief, bereavement, wonder, and love through the voice of poetry. Themes in her writings include parenting, gardening, the natural world, love, thriving and failure, grief, and daily life. She's been an organic fruit grower, a newspaper and magazine editor, and a parent educator for Parents as Teachers. She earned her MA in English Language & Linguistics at UW-Madison.

Her three-word mantra: *I'm still learning*, and, if limited to one: *Adjust*.

This book is set in Optima typeface, developed by the German type-designer and calligrapher Hermann Zapf. Its inspiration came during Zapf's first trip to Italy in 1950. While in Florence he visited the cemetery of the Basilica di Santa Croce and was immediately taken by the design of the lettering found on the old tombstones there. He quickly sketched an early draft of the design on a 1000 lire banknote, and after returning to Frankfurt devoted himself to its development. It was first released as Optima by the D. Stempel AG foundry in 1958 and shortly thereafter by Mergenthaler in the United States. Inspired by classical Roman inscriptions and distinguished by its flared terminals, this typeface is prized for its curves and straights which vary minutely in thickness, providing a graceful and clear impression to the eye.